THE HERMITAGE LANDSCAPE

THE HERMITAGE LANDSCAPE

BEFORE AND AFTER THE 1998 TORNADO

FLETCH COKE

FEATURING PHOTOGRAPHS
BY JOHN T. HOOPER

HILLSBORO PRESS
FRANKLIN, TENNESSEE

TENNESSEE HERITAGE LIBRARY
Bicentennial Collection

Printed in the United States of America

03   02   01   00   99   1   2   3   4   5

Library of Congress Catalog Card Number: 99-71675

ISBN: 1-57736-140-7

Cover design by Gary Bozeman

A portion of the proceeds from the sale of this book will benefit
the Ladies' Hermitage Association in their continuing effort to preserve and protect
The Hermitage, home of President Andrew Jackson.

Published by
HILLSBORO PRESS
an imprint of
PROVIDENCE HOUSE PUBLISHERS
238 Seaboard Lane • Franklin, Tennessee 37067
800-321-5692
www.providencehouse.com

CONTENTS

FROM THE REGENT

Andrew Jackson

Dear Interested Readers,

The Ladies' Hermitage Association has a long and proud history dating back to 1889 when a group of resistant women kept the state from turning Andrew Jackson's house into a home for indigent Confederate veterans. Members of the Jackson and Donelson families and other interested friends formed an organization patterned after the Mount Vernon Ladies' Association. Through the years, little by little, they repaired the house, reclaimed the land, reacquired most of the original furnishings and family relics, and returned the mansion to the way it was in 1837 when Andrew Jackson came from Washington.

Today, we continue this work (while recovering from a devastating tornado). I would share with you three areas of our hopes and dreams for the next ten years. One, there is a need for strengthening our financial resources: building an endowment fund; expanding our donor base; improving our rental facilities; and offering exclusive merchandise, reproductions, and publications. Two, we are working hard to protect the whole seven hundred acres from encroaching real estate and commercial development. Three, a new interpretive plan is being developed for restoring the property to the same conditions that existed while Jackson lived. There will be emphasis on the slave community, and on the interaction of all who lived and worked on the Hermitage property.

While undertaking these new initiatives, we continue our efforts to recover from the tornado of 1998. The Ladies' Hermitage Association and Hermitage staff have emerged from the storm with a renewed commitment to restoring the grandeur of Jackson's estate. It is our hope that this book will promote a clearer understanding of the impact of the storm on the Hermitage landscape and provide valuable information on recovering from disaster.

Honey Rodgers, Regent,
Ladies' Hermitage Association

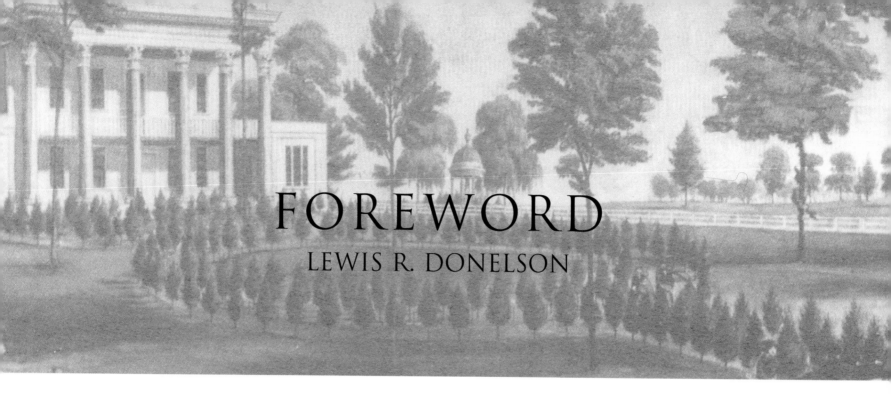

FOREWORD

LEWIS R. DONELSON

I was particularly honored and pleased when my cousin, Fletch Coke, asked me to write a foreword to her new book, *The Hermitage Landscape: Before and after the 1998 Tornado.*

My great-grandfather, Andrew Jackson Donelson, was raised by Rachel and Andrew Jackson at the original Hermitage. He served as Jackson's personal secretary, the equivalent of today's chief of staff, while Jackson was president, and he and his family lived in the White House with Andrew Jackson. My great-grandfather's home, Tulip Grove, was built the year before the present Hermitage was restored following the fire in 1834. My grandfather, the first Lewis Randolph Donelson, spent a substantial part of his younger years and finished high school while living at Tulip Grove. He later became one of the original trustees of The Hermitage. My father succeeded him and my brother succeeded my father and they served until the trustees were abolished and the ownership of the property was turned over in full to the Ladies' Hermitage Association (LHA) which had maintained it with great love and determination for so many years without any assistance from the State of Tennessee.

I can remember my first visit to The Hermitage in the 1920s as a young boy. My vivid memory is of the carriage, which was in an old shed in the back of the Hermitage in very poor condition. I was not sufficiently observant at the time to notice the general condition of the house, but I remember my father telling me of the struggles to maintain it by the Ladies. I also recall my brother recounting the Ladies' efforts to purchase surrounding acres to restore the plantation to its original size. There followed numerous visits over the years. I have taken the tour dozens of times and I remember how dark and Victorian the house appeared on those visits. It is a special joy for me to now see how bright, cheery, and inviting it was in Jackson's time. For anyone who hasn't seen it recently it is a different place and uplifts the spirit. The Ladies' Hermitage Association honored me by naming me co-chair of the Hermitage National Advisory Committtee. I am also privileged to serve with my cousin Fletch Coke on the Tennessee Presidents Trust, which supervises the presidential papers of our state's three presidents to maximize their educational and historical value.

I had the privilege of requesting the governor to put in the budget the first state appropriation for The Hermitage when the funds were raised for the Visitors Center and then I served as one of the honorary co-chairmen of the capital drive which raised the remainder of those funds. It has been a great privilege for me to see the results. The Hermitage, its grounds, and the Visitors Center are a magnificent public treasure, unique among presidential houses because the home contains most of the original furnishings and the remainder have been replaced with replicas of the originals. Several years back, plans, specifications, and detailed descriptions of the home as it was in Jackson's later years were discovered. As a result the home has been beautifully restored to the style and decorations of the period during which President Jackson lived in it following his presidency.

I was in Nashville at the time the tornado struck in 1998, on the seventeenth floor of the City Center Building, and it never occurred to me at the time that The Hermitage was being damaged. But the loss was unbelievable. It was over a month before I actually got out there to see it but at the time the large toppled trees were everywhere. Particularly distressing was the thought that the cedars along the guitar-shaped drive in front of the house which were planted by Andrew Jackson were mostly gone, and the tulip poplars which stood in front of Tulip Grove and in the whole grove between Tulip Grove and The Hermitage were decimated. These trees were large enough when President Martin Van Buren visited Tulip Grove in 1842 that he suggested the name Tulip Grove for the home. Many of the tulip poplars were over two hundred years old. Perhaps in one way the most damaging effect was to the peripheral trees which sheltered the property from nearby urban growth. Prior to the tornado, the Hermitage had been restored to what it must have been like in Andrew Jackson's time because visitors had no consciousness of the world outside. It was surrounded by trees as it must have been in Jackson's day—a beautiful rural setting. It will take many years to restore it to that pristine condition. We must do that.

The Hermitage is a unique retrospective of the national period of American history between the last of the Virginia presidential dynasty and the Civil War. It embodies a nation bursting with energy and growth, very agrarian in its economy but truly providing unlimited opportunity to every one of its citizens. Andrew Jackson rose from extremely limited circumstances to become the highest official in the land. The home and Jackson's life stand as a monument that America is the land of opportunity. With him the tradition began that every citizen in the United States, regardless of humble beginnings, could grow up to be president.

It is a special honor to be a part of this record of The Hermitage's recent trying time. I am confident we will restore the grounds superbly and this treasured national heritage will continue as a shrine to liberty and opportunity.

FOREWORD
DOUGLAS HENRY

The Hermitage has been a strong presence in my life since childhood. After election to the senate in 1970, there have been various occasions when I have been able to make an initiative for The Hermitage, generally of a financial nature, as needs have occurred from time to time. It is fitting for the state to appropriate for the benefit of The Hermitage; the property was acquired by the state in the last century and was later conveyed to the Ladies' Hermitage Association to be managed on behalf of Tennessee and her citizens. In fact, one statutory duty of the Association is to "keep the property in such state of preservation as the association may deem best so as to display the respect, love, and affection which a grateful state and people cherish for their illustrious hero and statesman, Andrew Jackson" (Tennessee Code Annotated, Section 4-13-102). In accord with that statutory charge, various governors have from time to time proposed funds in the annual state budget to assist The Hermitage. As chairman of the Senate Finance, Ways and Means Committee, it has been my privilege and pleasure to urge upon different administrations, and perhaps to play some part in, the proposal of funds for The Hermitage and the acceptance of those proposals by the legislature.

The part which The Hermitage has played in my life was stimulated by two of my ancestresses who were regents: my grandmother, Emily James Selph (Mrs. Robert Allison) Henry, and my mother, Kathryn Craig (Mrs. Douglas Selph) Henry. My grandmother was regent in 1922 and my mother was regent 1955–1957. In addition, my sister, Margaret Sinclair Henry (Mrs. William Wade) Wood, has served on the board.

Another connection to The Hermitage is through my wife, Loiette Hume Henry. Her great-great-great-grandfather was Dr. William Hume, who arrived from Scotland

ix

and became the second pastor of the First Presbyterian Church. In the course of his work there, he and General Jackson became friends and confidants. Their relationship culminated in Dr. Hume's baptism of the general, who had before that event not been of a church.

An aspect of The Hermitage which drew me was the home which Tennessee maintained there for Confederate veterans for many years.

Finally, I have been drawn to The Hermitage by the career of General Jackson himself. When he defeated General Pakenham at Chalmette, Louisiana, he brought the United States onto the world stage as a power to be reckoned with. By reason of his philosophical devotion to the common man, as opposed to men of privilege, General Jackson made life better for those who were subject to tyrants both in his day and later. My first visit to The Hermitage occurred during grade school; I have been there several times a year in recent years.

The fire which badly damaged the church occurred after my mother's regency, when she was to oversee its restoration. She spent a great deal of effort working with the architect, Mr. Hardie Bass, in restoring the building which stands as a complement to

and adjunct of the great mansion erected by General Jackson.

The debt which Tennessee owes to the Ladies' Hermitage Association is large and ongoing. The state could, of course, have managed the property directly, engaging a staff and appropriating some amount from year to year to keep it up. It is not likely that such management, with all regard to the intention of those managing, would have produced anything like the result which has been achieved by the tireless volunteer efforts of the Ladies' Hermitage Association. Not only are the mansion and grounds today equal or superior, I would guess, to their condition when General Jackson lived there, but also the taxpayers have been relieved of an annual and heavy burden by dint of the vigor and imaginativeness of the members of the LHA.

The Hermitage, I have no doubt, looks forward to a bright and flourishing future. Americans and visitors to our country seem to have an increasing appetite for American history. By reason of General Jackson's philosophy as president, an enormous number of Americans feel strongly drawn to him. I expect that number to increase and that any cavils of revisionists will have no effect upon the renown as an early shaper of the republic to which he is entitled. To many like me, he

will always be the victor of Chalmette who raises a deep patriotic sentiment, whether one agrees or disagrees with him in political philosophy. Although he is a treasure of the Western world, he is Tennessee's treasure. The setting maintained so elegantly by the Ladies' Hermitage Association will continue to draw not only admirers of the general, but large numbers of Americans and others who are anxious to see the splendid achievement which he carved out in the frontier days of our state and which the Ladies' Hermitage Association maintains to be admired both today and into the limitless future.

A more recent attraction of The Hermitage, in addition to its patriotic and touristic magnetisms, is the drawing of scholars both of archaeology and of the society of the southern states in General Jackson's time. Excavations around the buildings and grounds have yielded artifacts from which scholars have learned and are learning many previously unexplored aspects of how life was lived by all involved in a complete and self-contained farm of the times, of which The Hermitage was a fine example.

In summary, as the years pass, The Hermitage will more and more fulfill the expectations of the LHA, the staff, the visitors, and I am bold enough to say of General Jackson himself.

PREFACE

For many Nashvillians, Thursday, April 16, 1998, will never be forgotten. All day there were warnings and alerts about "tornadic activity." In late afternoon, a tornado struck metropolitan Nashville. All evening the local television stations continued to replay footage of the tornado's path of destruction in downtown Nashville and east Nashville. Everyone looked in horror at the wreckage. The next morning, my husband Bill and I departed for Memphis to attend the wedding of a friend's son. Not until Saturday did we learn there had been any damage on The Hermitage property.

Returning home Sunday, we drove immediately to Lebanon Pike, stopping in front of the old Hermitage Church and Tulip Grove. What a dreadful sight! Entrances to The Hermitage grounds were closed. The following day, Bill and I toured the grounds with Executive Director Jim Vaughan and Bunny Blackburn. I felt a tremendous sense of loss. Having served on the Ladies' Hermitage Association Board 1977–1990, as regent 1987–1989, and as chairman of the mansion and garden restoration committees, the grounds at The Hermitage were as familiar to me as my own backyard. My first thought was the

need to contact professional photographer John Hooper and ask him to take on-site and aerial photographs. On Friday, one week plus one day, John began a series of photographs, recording the devastation on The Hermitage property. Many of those images are included in this book.

Anyone who has visited The Hermitage over the years can remember the large cedars arching over the driveway, the magnolias shading the tomb, and the majestic poplars standing in the lawns of Tulip Grove. On April 16, 1998, in less than one minute, these scenic views were changed forever.

Above—*Mrs. Ellen Stokes Wemyss, LHA board member and past Regent, and Mark Provost plant a new willow tree at the garden gate in 1989.* LHA

This is a book about the Hermitage landscape before and after the April 1998 tornado. This is not a book about the mansion, its current restoration, or about Andrew Jackson's military or political careers. Here we will focus on the out-of-doors. What did people see and record about their visits to The Hermitage? We will look in the letters, journals, and diaries of those who lived there and those who visited. What could eyewitnesses tell about their experiences on the day of the tornado? Excerpts from oral history interviews, conducted by the author with staff and board members, will give the reader an inside look at their responses to this emergency and their impressions following the storm. Prints and photographs will reveal the growth and change on the Hermitage grounds. Photographs of the tornado damage will explain the extent of the loss from the storm. Let us be thankful that no one was injured in the wretched minute of the twister. And let us be grateful that the mansion, the tomb, Tulip Grove, and the church were spared.

Lost during the tornado were 1,234 trees on the historic grounds around the mansion, in the garden, in the adjacent fields, and on the lawns of Tulip Grove and the church. Some of these trees were standing when President Jackson lived at The Hermitage—some were even older. Many of the destroyed trees had been planted since 1889, when the LHA took over management. Fortunately most of the young trees, planted during the past twenty years, sustained the winds and will be the trees to flourish in the years to come.

We should take heart from what Andrew Jackson, having been told of the frost damage to the grounds of his home, wrote from Washington to Sarah York Jackson, his daughter-in-law, at The Hermitage:

I sincerely regret the ravages made by the frost in the garden and particularly that the willow at the garden gate is destroyed. This I wish you to replace.
Andrew Jackson, May 19, 1832

A month later, President Jackson again wrote Sarah. This time he expressed his delight that the willow was putting forth from its roots. Jackson's attitude was practical. The important matter was to replant when necessary. Landscape planning is presently underway at The Hermitage. New trees will be planted. Over time, the emptiness and openness caused by the loss of the trees will be softened.

Like Andrew Jackson, the LHA will plant trees for the future.

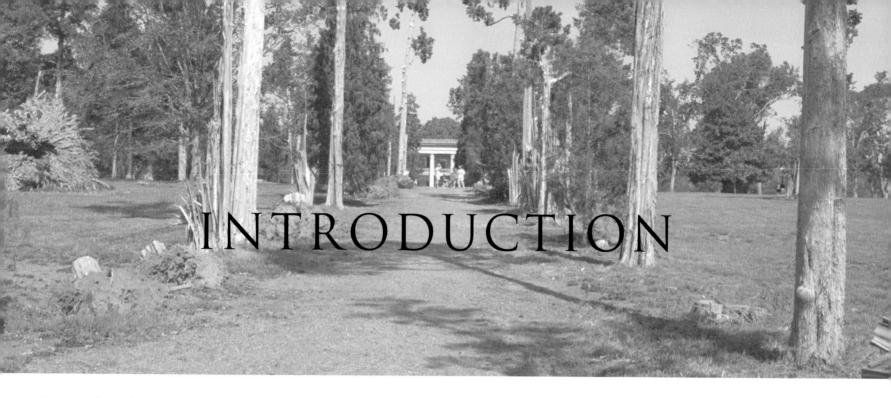

INTRODUCTION

In a normal year, the entire state of Tennessee records an average of twelve tornadoes. On April 16, 1998, there were eleven tornadoes reported in the Middle Tennessee area alone.

On the afternoon of April 16, 1998, The Hermitage was bustling with over two hundred visitors, including busloads of school children from Memphis and East Tennessee. Visitors and staff were located in numerous places on the property, including the Visitors Center, mansion, garden, tomb area, Tulip Grove, and pathways.

April 16, 1998

Morning

I woke up early that morning because of thunderstorms. When I came downstairs all three networks were already 100 percent weather forecasting. When I came to work, we have a weather radio that goes off every time there is an alert. It went off continuously all morning announcing thunderstorms or severe storm warnings, tornado warnings, tornado alerts.

Jim Vaughan,
executive director

Midday

And each time that the alert went off, we would go into the old board room, next to my office [Administration Building] and turn on one of the local TV stations so that we could see the track where that particular storm was projected.

Jim Vaughan,
executive director

Afternoon

3:15 P.M.

About 3:15, they were forecasting a storm to come directly to Nashville and to hit Lakewood, a few miles up the road from us. At that point I asked Angie to take the radio and go to the mansion, and Larry Hitchcock, who is our deputy chief of security, to go to the Andrew Jackson Center. We met briefly and decided if this does not change direction in fifteen minutes then let's get everybody to safety. Larry and I agreed that everybody at the Andrew Jackson Center should be brought from the store and the café into the theater, the only big room without any windows. Angie would make sure that everyone in the mansion would get into the basement. We agreed to radio Tulip Grove and tell them to get into the basement.

Jim Vaughan,
executive director

3:20 P.M.

I ran to the mansion and took the keys from the interpreters, went down and unlocked the cellar door. Then I went back up and waited for Jim to radio which he did, saying that we should move everybody. I went out in the main hall of the mansion and I remember thinking "Don't say 'tornado.' Don't cause hysteria." I just said that we had severe weather and that we were asking everyone to move to the cellar.

Angie Nichols,
executive assistant

3:30 P.M.

I arrived at The Hermitage about 3:15 that afternoon. Mr. Vaughan wanted to see me. I went to the Administration Building and he told me that the weather was very unstable and that we needed to keep an eye on it. I said that I agreed with him. While we were standing there talking, approximately 3:30 P.M., the local TV station issued a tornado warning, giving the track of this storm coming through Donelson which would be in the Hermitage area at approximately 3:45 P.M. So we had fifteen minutes.

Larry Hitchcock,
deputy chief of security

I was in the mansion that day. I had not heard most of the weather reports. They were talking about storms and thunderstorms headed our way, but I never thought much about it. About 3:30 P.M., Angie came up to the house and she told me that we may have to go to the cellar pretty quickly. In a few minutes, she said we have to go now. We told the visitors. We opened the cellar doors and turned on the lights. The visitors immediately started filing down there. When we got the house cleared and the doors closed, I went to the Cabin by the Spring and got two ladies and walked them back up. Even then, I thought this was absolutely silly—that we are going to stand in the basement for ten or fifteen minutes and it may rain.

John Lamb,
lead interpreter

On the day of the tornado, we were in the midst of a very busy afternoon in the museum store. People were very hesitant about leaving when we told them they had to. We told them we wanted to take them to safety away from the glass. And they asked, "Can't we buy our things?"

Barbara Nance,
assistant manager of the museum store

And about 3:30, I radioed to them that they better get to shelter. That was just about the time that the TV went off the air because the storm had hit Nashville.

Jim Vaughan,
executive director

3:35 P.M.

And all the interpreters were helping me. One went outside and got the people on the back porch. And we all filed down. And it was not raining and the wind was not blowing. And we were a good ten minutes before it hit the property. And I remember the visitors joking, as we were filing down, like "This is not on the normal tour." And "Are you all sure something is coming?" and "Is this necessary?" I think they thought we were being overly cautious. After everyone got down in the cellar, my immediate thought was "Did we get everybody on the grounds?" A security officer came up about that time. He covered the backyard and I went around the front, and looked out in the garden. We were trying to make sure that no one was left on the grounds. We came back to the cellar. Just as the wind picked up, the electricity went off.

Angie Nichols,
executive assistant

3:40 P.M.

Kristin and I were in the garden. Stan, one of the guards, came around and told us that we needed to take cover. We started walking across to the basement of the Administration Building. I remember thinking, "Who's throwing golf balls at us?" Golf balls were hitting the ground. I could not imagine what it was. Kristin is from Ohio and she said usually when a tornado is coming, you have hail. And that's what this was—big old hailstones.

Karen Danielson,
gardener

We went out to the employee parking lot, right outside the Administration Building. We looked to the west and there was this wall of very dark scary looking clouds coming towards us. We could not see anything that looked like a funnel cloud. There was this curtain of clouds headed towards us. As it got closer, we began to see this debris, way up in the air, with roofing tin and branches. Then I realized this was the real thing.

Larry McKee,
staff archaeologist

Tony Guzzi and I actually opened the back door at the Visitors Center and watched the tornado coming towards us. I have been places where tornadoes were ten or fifteen miles away, but I have never been some place where I actually watched one coming and could experience things like the pressure dropping and your ears popping. And the ominous feeling of something like that coming straight at you. As soon as we felt that pressure dropping and you could see the clouds going straight up in the air, we both kind of looked at each other and said it's time to shut the door and get inside.

Mark Kindy,
coordinator of historical interpreters

Within five minutes of hearing that a tornado was coming through, we were all back on the floor in the Collections Department at the Andrew Jackson Center. There was an outside door. We opened the door once. The clouds were a greenish color. You could see something was going on. . . . That some kind of storm was coming. It got really loud and then it got quiet. It happened within five minutes.

Anna Christ,
development assistant
and membership coordinator

3:42 P.M.

At 3:40, everybody in the area of the Visitors Center was in the auditorium. Shelly and I walked back outside about 3:42. We looked back toward the baseball field, and Shelly made a remark, you could see clouds swirling around. . . . "There it is." I agreed with her. We went back inside.

Larry Hitchcock,
deputy chief of security

About 3:40, Larry, Mark, Janie, and I stood out on the sidewalk and watched the winds pick up and we could literally see the tornado coming over the hill. We ducked in the basement of the Administration Building. And we were probably in the basement not more than a minute and half, maybe only a minute.

Jim Vaughan,
executive director

I was in the Education Building. My son had just come over from school. Mr. Vaughan said we needed to take shelter. So we all went out into the parking lot by the building. People started to flock out there. There must have been about ten adults in the group and we watched the tornado come up. It was huge. Huge. It reminded me of the thing that was hovering over the city in the *Independence Day* movie. It was tremendous. And we just stood out there, just like a bunch of dummies . . . watching it get closer and closer and closer. Finally the sky started to turn yellow. We're all standing there with our mouths hanging open, like I can't believe this is really happening. Then my son said, "Grown-ups, I think it's time for us to go to shelter." We just barely made it.

Janie Carder,
education coordinator

In the auditorium, it sounded like the Jolly Green Giant out there. Thud. Thud. Thud. But I had no idea it was the trees going down. The steel doors were heaving.

Barbara Nance,
assistant manager of museum store

It looked so funny with all these people gathering round and looking up at you. The interpreters, Angie, and a guard were with us. They closed the cellar doors and almost immediately the lights went out. When the lights went out, the alarms came on in the mansion so the cellar is blaring with these alarms. The lights are out, so it is completely pitch dark down there. Everybody is kind of chattering. But even so, I do not think that we were all that scared.

John Lamb,
lead interpreter

Every alarm in the cellar in the mansion starts beeping and squealing. I have about forty or fifty people in a hot basement in the dark, with alarms squealing, red lights flashing, Stan kept trying to keep the cellar door open for air as long as possible. When the wind picked up really hard, he pulled the door and almost immediately the tree fell on it. He really waited till the last minute as

long as he could. You heard it and you saw the leaves coming through the cracks of the door.

Angie Nichols,
executive assistant

I was here on the day of the tornado. It was between 3:30 and 3:45 when the storm hit. I was near the service road behind the Administration Building watching it there as it came across the parking lot, looking from the Administration Building across the bus parking lot by the Andrew Jackson Center. It was getting real real dark, debris in the air. I watched it until it was right on top of us. Then a big limb broke off a tree near the Administration Building. It only lasted a matter of seconds.

Jim Clark,
buildings and maintenance supervisor

PART ONE

The Hermitage, twelve miles from downtown Nashville, Tennessee, is a National Historic Landmark. The home of Andrew Jackson, seventh president of the United States, is visited annually by thousands of people. For over one hundred years, the site has been managed by the Ladies' Hermitage Association.

What makes The Hermitage unique? Probably foremost is the person who lived there. Andrew Jackson was born on the frontier of South Carolina in 1767. His parents had arrived as immigrants from Ulster (Northern Ireland) only two years prior to his birth. He was determined to be educated and to be successful. After studying law, he moved to Nashville, on the bluffs of the Cumberland River. He took lodgings at the Widow Donelson's place. Her daughter, unhappily married, returned to her mother's home and there met and fell in love with Andrew Jackson. He was fortunate because the Donelson family was large and prominent in the early days of Middle Tennessee.

The Jacksons moved to The Hermitage farm in 1804. After residing for almost seventeen years in a two-story log building, they moved into their new Federal-style brick house. To the Jacksons, "The Hermitage" meant the house plus the orchards, garden, wood lots, outbuildings, barns, and fields—the place. Apparently Rachel chose the location for the residence because when this house, with some additions, partially burned in 1834, Jackson refused to consider rebuilding at a different spot. After the fire, the house was rebuilt. The mansion looks today virtually the same as when completed in 1836. This is the present mansion.

A great many people visited The Hermitage during Jackson's lifetime. After his death in 1845, The Hermitage became a place of pilgrimage. The 1,050-acre farm

1

was inherited by Andrew Jackson Jr. When financial difficulties forced him to sell, luckily the State of Tennessee saw fit to buy. To be commended are Governor Andrew Johnson and the legislature for agreeing in 1856 to purchase five hundred acres of The Hermitage farm, for which they paid the impressive sum of $48,000.

A second threat came in 1889 when the legislature was considering a bill to convert the mansion into a home for indigent Confederate veterans. The Ladies' Hermitage Association was chartered. The state approved that twenty-five acres including the mansion and the tomb be managed by the LHA. Over the years, the state has authorized that the remainder of the five hundred acres come under the LHA's management.

To preserve, protect, and restore have been the aims of the LHA for the mansion, the tomb, the other buildings, the garden, the fields, and the forests. Maintaining the older trees and the planting of new trees have been objectives from the beginning. In recent years, there have been a good many trees lost to age, to lightning, to storms. New trees were being planted in their places. And then—the tornado of 1998!

The Entrance

Until the mid-1980s, visitors to The Hermitage turned off Lebanon Pike onto Rachel's Lane. When the State of Tennessee closed this entrance to the grounds, the present entry was constructed from Old Hickory Boulevard. Today Rachel's Lane is a quiet country road connecting The Hermitage with Tulip Grove and the church. An underpass takes travelers under Lebanon Pike. Until the tornado, Rachel's Lane was grown up with old cedars and maples lining the split-rail fences on either side. In recent years, many new trees had been planted along the lane between the old trees. Fortunately these young trees survived the tornado.

In 1843, two years before Jackson's death, Thomas L. Jones, on seeing the residence from the turnpike, enthused over its "distinguished appearance." He and several companions discussed what they should do:

> Never having seen the veteran Hero, we could not resist the temptation to call. Entering the wide lane that led down in front of the house, we shortly arrived at a large gate. . . . Having debated some little time whether or not it would be proper to enter this gate on horseback, we determined to do so, and rode boldly up. . . .
>
> Thomas L. Jones,
> November 18, 1843

Andrew Jackson returned home from Washington, at the end of his second term, in the spring of 1837. The next year, Ralph E. W. Earl drew the design and laid off the guitar-shaped carriage drive in front of the mansion. The shape may have been suggested by Sarah York Jackson, the president's daughter-in-law, who played a guitar (which is still in the parlor of the Hermitage today). Earl, painter of many portraits of Jackson as well as Jackson's friend, was residing at the Hermitage that summer.

In 1851, Rev. C. C. Jones visited The Hermitage in company with Rev. John Todd Edgar of First Presbyterian Church, Nashville. Dr. Edgar had preached Andrew Jackson's funeral on June 10, 1845.

> An iron gate let us into the lawn immediately before the mansion; nor had we in our approach seen anything more than the top of a chimney or the glimpse of a wall or pillar; nor did we see anything now, so embosomed is it in trees, and so full of small cedars and shrubbery is the lawn. The road winds around an enclosed plat in shape of a guitar.
>
> Rev. C. C. Jones,
> June 5, 1851

Protection of the cedars on the carriage drive was a concern in the early days of the LHA management. By 1910, the LHA had passed a policy that any cedar lost to age or storm on the driveway would be replaced so that the guitar-shaped design would be maintained.

In the summer of 1914, the LHA had to deal with the borers, little moths which were causing considerable harm to the cedar trees in the driveway. The "Tree Doctor" put an end to the damage.

By carriage, the trip of twelve miles to The Hermitage from the city of Nashville took at least two hours. Many were awestruck on arrival.

> We came to the iron gate which was standing hospitably open. Slowly our old fat mules turned into the gate up the graveled driveway. We sat in perfect silence. Being the first visit to this place, it was very impressive and we were hushed into silence and thrilled with the contemplation of it.
>
> Julia Organ Rider,
> September 1, 1914

The LHA Board voted, in August 1921, to make the front gates closed to traffic to reduce injury to the old cedar trees along the driveway. Unfortunately, a tornado in March 1923 destroyed sixty-three trees on the grounds. At the LHA Board meeting the next month, Mrs. Granbery Jackson proposed that cigar boxes be made from the wood of the fallen trees. Mrs. Bettie M. Donelson suggested that since Jackson

Above—*A close-up view of the west side of the Hermitage mansion, 1885.* LHA

smoked a pipe, tobacco boxes should be made. Both these suggestions were accepted.

Before the 1998 tornado, visitors often walked the length of the driveway to the front gate and experienced the shade of the overarching cedars. For special occasions, the front gates have been opened so that visitors could walk from Rachel's Lane to the mansion. During the celebration of Jackson's two-hundredth birthday, March 15, 1967, President Lyndon Johnson walked up the driveway while Mrs. Johnson rode in Jackson's original carriage to the mansion, where they had breakfast in the dining room.

3

During the Civil War, the Federal Army occupied Nashville from February 1862 until the close of the conflict. To protect the former home of President Jackson and its residents, at certain times during the war years a federal guard was posted on the place. Many federal soldiers made a trip to The Hermitage.

The Hermitage is a few hundred yards from the main turnpike—is reached through a narrow well traversed lane which leads immediately to the iron gate in front of the extensive lawn, surrounding the mansion.

Federal soldier, November 23, 1862

J. Bucy and I had gotten in the car. . . . We could not get out of the parking lot. Both ways on Rachel's Lane were blocked. Twenty feet up were piles of trees.

Anna Christ, development assistant

All the trees that formed a sort of canopy on Rachel's Lane were all gone. Like someone had taken a chain saw and had chopped them down on both sides of the lane.

Andrew Jackson VI, great-great-great grandson of the president

Looking up Rachel's Lane . . . it was solid tree trunks . . . there were big massive trees crisscrossing down. All the trees on the right fell across the road and all the trees on the left fell across the road.

Marianne M. Byrd, LHA Secretary, 1997–1998

Above—*Aerial view from 1,000 feet; looking from Rachel's Lane toward the Hermitage mansion, fallen cedars crisscrossed the carriage drive. Cleanup had already been completed in the garden. 4/24/98.* JTH

Opposite, top—*The cleanup squad had to deal with huge trees and upturned fences on Rachel's Lane. 6/1/98.* JTH

Opposite, inset—*New split-rail fences along Rachel's Lane in the spring of 1989.* FC

Opposite, bottom left—*Lone automobile on Rachel's Lane, 1905.* LHA

Opposite, bottom right—*Early morning, the day after the tornado. One lane of the road was partially cleared after fallen trees had blocked Rachel's Lane in both directions the day before. 4/17/98.* KD

5

Opposite—*Four photographs reveal the damage at the front gates of The Hermitage. Remarkably the gatepost stood firm. Fence sections were upended by the root of a tree. 4/24/98.* JTH

Opposite, inset—*Three children appear to be waiting for the gates to open. The cedars looked like soldiers in parade formation, 1904.* LHA

Above—*The gates are open for a horse drawn carriage to depart, early 1880s.* NR

Sam Houston and a friend from Paris, Tennessee, visited General and Mrs. Jackson in 1825. The friend wrote up his impressions for the local newspaper:

We halted in front of a large gate, which led into a yard covered with blue grass and shaded by black locusts, to a spacious brick building, nearly in the form of a square. On entering the gate, we discovered the old veteran sitting on the porch, reading.

Tennessee gentleman,
June 19, 1825

James, the gardener, and a couple of other folks on the tractor were clearing the trees on Rachel's Lane. Channel 5 was filming the view from the lane up to the mansion. That is the shot with a tree laying on the pillar and the fence just practically wiped out from the different trees. And that was hard. Even the news folks felt it. They realized the impact of what they were seeing. . . . Even the people clearing the lane were realizing the devastation throughout the property.

J. Bucy,
sales manager

7

In the 1860s, visitors often commented on the tall cedars, sugar trees, hickory, and ash in the front lawn. In 1872, a visitor described the cedar carriage drive:

The front of the Hermitage is approached by an avenue of cedars, the boughs of which meet overhead and form a continuous archway to within a short distance of the house, where it opens into a small court interspersed with deciduous trees.

Nashville Union & American,
January 7, 1872

The biggest change that comes to mind is the front lawn of the mansion with all the cedars gone. That looks the most drastically different. There is no buffer zone where there was before. That is one of the most devastating things.

Anna Christ,
development assistant and
membership coordinator

Opposite—*Majestic cedars lined the carriage drive in 1894.* TSLA

Opposite, inset top—*In this 1970s aerial, the lush growth of the cedars hid the shape of the carriage drive.* LHA

Opposite, inset bottom—*On Jackson's 200th birthday, Mrs. Lyndon B. Johnson (in the carriage) and the president (on foot) made their way to the mansion for breakfast.* Vic Cooley.TSLA

Above—*Grim reminders of the force of the tornado. In the distance on the left, the downed beech tree. 9/26/98.* JTH

Right—*Cedars fell to left and to right across the drive. 6/1/98.* JTH

Opposite, far left—*From the air, the outline of the guitar-shaped drive was revealed by the destruction of the cedars. 4/24/98.* JTH

Opposite, top; and opposite, bottom left—*Few changes are noticeable in these two views, top 1880s and bottom 1990s.* LHA

Above; left; and opposite, bottom right—*How close the mansion came to the tornado's fury can be seen in these three views. 5/5/98* JTH

Shortly after the tornado, when I was on the front lawn, I could not find my way around. I could not see anything as a point of reference, where I could tell where I was and which way I was headed. The trees were everywhere. I could not get my bearings.

Janie Carder, education coordinator

It is sad about the trees. The trees are a big part of the history of this place. When you consider that one of the trees in the front yard could have been older than the state of Tennessee itself. The sad part about any tornado in any community is that it usually gets the older trees, the ones that if they could talk, what would they tell you. Those are gone now. And we are left with the smaller, younger trees.

Mark Kindy,
coordinator of historical interpreters

When I came up in the middle of May, the front yard was still filled with trees, fallen trees, up over your head. We walked up from the Visitors Center . . . and made a circle through the trees that had fallen down. From the front lawn, you could not see the Hermitage itself or the garden or the tomb. You *could* see Lebanon Road. I had never seen that road before from the Hermitage. All those trees that blocked the view of the road were gone.

Andrew Jackson VI

As we reached the rise above the Visitors Center, we could see all the trees down. We just took off running. You had to jump over things and climb over trees. Our first concern was the mansion. We were pretty pleased that it was still standing up. I felt great relief when I saw the inside of the mansion and saw that it was fine.

Marsha Mullin,
curator of collections

When I arrived, it made me feel real sick for being here as long as I have. I did not know what shape the mansion or the other buildings were in when I arrived. We had eleven officers and we worked twelve-hour shifts all through that time, for two weeks. It was two weeks before electrical power was restored. And telephone service did not return for three weeks.

W. T. Henderson,
chief of security

Above, top—*LHA Board and Jim Vaughan, executive director, gathered in August 1998, at the root of the beech tree on the front lawn.* AC

Above—*LHA Board members joined T. L. Baker, curator, who was standing in a tree crater. A tornado toppled sixty-three trees on March 11, 1923.* LHA.

Right—*The oldest beech tree in Davidson County, Tennessee, was one of the 1,234 victims in the 1998 tornado at The Hermitage. 5/5/98.* JTH

Right, inset—*People inspecting the damage are almost lost in the tangle of branches heaped about the front lawn. 5/5/98.* JTH

The trees on the west side of the driveway fell east. And the trees on the east side of the driveway fell west. The big beech tree in the front lawn fell northwest toward the mansion.

Raymond Johnson,
co-chief of security

The front driveway looked like you dropped a box of toothpicks. And they scrambled every which way. There was no pattern at all.

W. T. Henderson,
chief of security

Rachel's Lane down to the main road (Old Hickory Boulevard) was completely blocked with fallen trees. Mr. Vaughan contacted the Maintenance Department and they got the chain saws and the tractors. It took approximately two hours to get the lane open so that people could leave here.

A couple of hours after the storm, I walked up to the mansion. It was total devastation. There were limbs, trees everywhere. You had to climb through trees to get to the front porch. It looked like a war zone. Terrible.

Larry Hitchcock,
deputy chief of security

PART TWO

After living seventeen years in the log building on The Hermitage farm, Rachel and Andrew Jackson moved to their new Federal-style brick residence in 1821. This was the house which Rachel knew.

The Garden

In September 1827, a visitor, Juliana Conner, described a walk through the garden:

After I was rested, Rachel proposed walking into the garden, which is very large and quite her hobby. I never saw anyone more enthusiastically fond of flowers. She culled for me the only rose which was in bloom and made up a pretty nosegay; after an agreeable stroll we returned to the drawing room. . . . Mrs. Jackson would not permit me to go without a bouquet, which she arranged tastily.

Juliana Conner,
September 4, 1827

On December 22, 1828, Andrew Jackson wrote to his friend, General Richard K. Call, in Tallahassee, Florida, "Mrs. J was a few days past, suddenly, & violently, attacked, with pains in her left shoulder & breast and such the contraction of the breast, that suffocation was apprehended before the necessary aid could be afforded." Jackson expected to depart for Washington between the tenth and fifteenth of January but, he emphasized to General Call, "I cannot leave her, believing as I do, that my separating from her would destroy her, and the persecution she has suffered, has endeared her more if possible than ever, to me." Mrs. Jackson died the evening this letter was written.

On Christmas Eve, Rachel Jackson was buried in the southeast corner of her garden. The next spring, Ralph E.W. Earl, portrait painter and friend of the family, wrote to President Jackson that the overseer at The Hermitage was building "a new

15

house over the tomb of Mrs. Jackson," with three windows and a folding door, to be painted white. Earl also added, "the four willows that you planted are all growing finely." This house protected Rachel's grave for the next four years.

Eight months after his wife's death the president wrote to his son, inquiring about the condition of the willows and flowers planted around her grave:

My Dear son inform me on this subject, you know it is the one dearest to my heart, and her memory will remain fresh there as long as life lasts.

Andrew Jackson,
August 20, 1829

From Washington City, President Jackson's letters were full of anguish over the care of the garden and her grave. To his nephew, Samuel Jackson Hays, he wrote in April 1830:

That garden is now to me a consecrated spot and I wish it carefully attended to, particularly the square around the sacred Tomb.

Andrew Jackson,
April 19, 1830

The following month, Samuel Jackson Hays was able to report to the president "The garden we found in fine order—the sides of the walks handsomely paved with brick and every thing looking very luxuriant and fine."

The president's letters home were filled with urgent requests for improvements. In 1831, Jackson wrote to his son to find out if some hickory nuts had been planted around Rachel's grave. A line of hickory trees, probably from these original nuts, grew up along the garden fence behind the tomb. The trees flourished. By 1897, it was reported at the LHA Board meeting, "the hickory trees in the garden near the tomb were very crowded and some of them would have to be cut to save the others."

In 1833, Nashville architect David Morison completed his commission to the president to design and build a "temple and monument" over Rachel's grave. This Doric circular-columned structure, with a copper roof, replaced the wooden grave house. At the same time, Morison was engaged in making improvements to the original brick house, adding wings and a one-story Greek Revival colonnade.

Maintenance of the garden, however, was uneven and Jackson's friend, William B. Lewis, had to write the president in April 1833, "the yard and garden look badly" and he had told the overseer that "the walks, border and squares must all be cleaned and kept so." The overseer promised to pay more attention. The president rejoiced in a letter to his son in May 1835:

How I am delighted to hear that the garden has regained its former appearance that it always possessed whilst your dear mother was living and that just attention is now paid to her monument. This is truly pleasing to me and is precisely as it ought to be.

Andrew Jackson,
May 1, 1835

In the spring of 1837, at the end of his second term as president, Jackson returned to The Hermitage from Washington City. In November, a visitor, Mr. N. Lester, described walking through the garden, "tastefully laid off in plats, ornamented with various kinds of flowers and shrubbery," to the tomb which was surrounded "by rose bushes and the weeping willow."

Rachel Jackson Lawrence recalled that every afternoon, about sunset, her grandfather would walk to the garden to visit the grave of his beloved Rachel.

In 1838, Ralph E. W. Earl died at The Hermitage, and was the first person to be buried in the cemetery plot near the tomb. On June 8, 1845, "Old Hickory," seventy-eight years old, died and two days later he was buried beside his wife in the garden. From all over Tennessee, thousands of people journeyed to his funeral. Pilgrimages to the tomb of President and Mrs. Jackson continue today.

Many family members have been buried in the cemetery at The Hermitage, including Andrew Jackson Jr., his wife Sarah, their children, and many grandchildren. The most recent interment, in 1971, was the president's great-granddaughter, Marion Lawrence Symmes.

In 1851, six years after the president's death, Mary Elizabeth Lewis Dufield, on an afternoon visit, described the center flower beds as "one solid bed of verbena, pinks, tulips, pinys [peonies] and other flowers too tedious to mention and too beautiful for me to attempt a description."

Sarah York Jackson and her sister Marion Adams were quite involved with the garden. Sarah wrote to her daughter, Rachel, away at school in April 1852, of a very cold winter and the loss of early flowers and yet "we have had a supply of fine roses. We have now about fifty varieties of roses."

A visitor in 1856 observed that there were "two or three weeping willows and four beautiful magnolia trees standing near and shading the tomb."

By the 1870s, a visitor noticed "a thick grove of magnolias stood densely matted together, forming a leafy screen through which we passed to a small circular temple."

During the Civil War and the difficult years following, the State of Tennessee lacked sufficient funds to care for Jackson's old home place. A committee, appointed by the state legislature, visited The Hermitage in February 1883 and discovered the house in "bad condition" and "the canopy over the tomb weather beaten and decaying, exposing the superstructure of the vault." An iron railing was quickly put in place to protect the tomb from souvenir hunters.

The LHA and the Garden

The garden and the tomb would continue to see inadequate care until the formation of the Ladies' Hermitage Association in 1889. Some of their earliest efforts were to restore the beauty of the garden. In May 1891, a report was made on "the successful propagation of small willows from those around the tomb" so that the decayed trees could be replaced.

On the occasion of Andrew Jackson's 130th birthday, Mrs. Mary L. Baxter reported to the LHA membership about the work of Mr. T. L. Baker, the curator:

The Curator did all the work of the place. He had covered the barn, repaired the Spring House, graded the lawn, filled the unsightly gullies, grubbed up sprouts, removed and rebuilt the fences on the East and West sides, had worked the garden, replacing all the [missing] brick, seeded the place in grass, and done all the work that was necessary to be done to keep the place in order.

Work had been done that an architect had said would cost $8,000 to do, and the outlay had been just $1,254.

Mrs. Mary L. Baxter,
March 15, 1897,
LHA Regent 1889-1899

The early days were not easy for the LHA. Money was scarce. Sometimes funds came from unexpected sources. President Theodore Roosevelt visited The Hermitage in 1907, and was decidedly upset with the condition of the place. Through his efforts, a Federal appropriation was made to the LHA. One of the projects funded was the covering of the garden walks with gravel. At the time, the LHA was only permitted by the State to charge twenty-five cents per visitor. The sale of peonies—a whole wagon load—in front of Meador's Shoe Store on Union Street took place on May 14, 1910. The local newspaper encouraged "the patronage of friends and the public." Caution was the watchword in spending:

The Regent has agreed to pay Mr. Polk, the old man who works in the garden, 90 cents a day in winter for every working day and $1.00 in summer. This was ratified by the Board. Wages have increased with the advance in everything else.

LHA minutes,
October 4, 1911

THE HERMITAGE LANDSCAPE

For many years, ceremonies have been held by the Ladies' Hermitage Association at the tomb in commemoration of the Battle of New Orleans, January 8, and in honor of Andrew Jackson's birthday, March 15. On the 200th anniversary of Jackson's birth, in 1967, President and Mrs. Lyndon B. Johnson paid a visit to The Hermitage and laid a wreath at the tomb.

Through droughts and excessive heat, through snowstorms and sleet, especially the blizzard of 1951, the Ladies' Hermitage Association has been dedicated to the beautification of the one-acre garden. Over the years, the tomb has been carefully restored, archaeological investigation has located original fence lines, and garden fences have been renewed. The ice storm of 1994 severely damaged one of the two remaining magnolias which then had to be removed. The tornado in 1998 destroyed the last magnolia, the hickories, and the other trees within and around the garden. Remarkably the tomb was not struck by any falling trees. A sunnier garden is the result of the loss of trees. The garden was still beautiful even during the first summer after the tornado.

Opposite—*A young lady surrounded by the beauty of the garden in 1917.* LHA

Left—*On June 21, 1910, a barbecue was given by the LHA for visiting Secretary of War J. M. Dickinson, in the center between two ladies in white dresses. Tables had been set along the garden fence.* M.W. Wiles. LHA

Above—*Ladies in the center of the garden. Second and third from the left, Mrs. Bettie M. Donelson, Regent, and Mrs. B. F. Wilson, Garden Chairman, 1919.* TSLA

On the morning after the tornado, my husband Andrew and I worked in the garden. What was amazing was that every tree around the garden had fallen into the garden. The cedar trees from the driveway had fallen into the garden, the cedar trees and magnolia inside the garden had fallen across each other, and the hickories, along the fence, had uprooted and fallen into the garden. The tornado must have gone right over the tomb. No damage to the tomb. Not a scratch.

Marianne M. Byrd,
LHA Secretary, 1997–1998

We were so behind in our weeding in the garden because we had all been lumberjacks for weeks. Cheekwood sent out fifteen or twenty of their gardeners. It was wonderful.

Karen Danielson,
gardener

Above—*At the garden gate in 1989. Towering trees blocked the view of the tomb in the southeast corner of the garden.* FC

Right—*Cheekwood Botanical Gardens, Nashville, sent out gardeners to help with the weeding after the tornado. Sections of a newly installed capped picket fence were destroyed. 5/5/98.* JTH

Right, inset—*Springtime view down the garden path to the gate in 1989.* FC

Opposite—*A lone snag of a tree stands watch over the tomb. The Hermitage gardeners worked diligently during the summer of 1998 to encourage the bloom of the flowers, roses, and crepe myrtles. 9/26/98.* JTH

Jackson sleeps in his own garden, in silence and apparent neglect. A weeping willow bends mournfully over the tomb. The garden paths are tangled and the summer-houses falling into decay. . . . I was shocked to observe the air of neglect and decay that pervaded The Hermitage in all its grounds.

Charles C. Jones,
June 21, 1859

To explain this neglect, Charles C. Jones told his parents that The Hermitage had passed out of the hands of the Jackson family and been sold to the State of Tennessee.

The place that touches the heart most is the garden. Tall trees are in the left side of it, but to the right, out where the sun shines are wide winding graveled paths, between beds of varicolored and brilliant-hued flowers and blooming shrubbery and vines were rioting in mingled grace and beauty. On a sudden bend in the walk was the tomb.

Julia Organ Rider,
September 1, 1914

Lith of Wagner & McGuigan, 100 Chesnut St. Phila.

TOMB OF GEN.ˡ ANDREW JACKSON,

12, MILES FROM NASHVILLE, TENN.ᴱ

Taken at the Spot on the day of his burial, June 10ᵗʰ 1845.

Born March 16ᵗʰ 1767. Died June 8ᵗʰ 1845.

Lithograph, Wagner & McGuigan, 100 Chesnut St., Philadelphia. 1845. Private Collection

Left—*Alfred Jackson, the guide at The Hermitage from 1889 until his death in 1901, is seen with a group of visitors inside the railing at the tomb, ca. 1890s.* A.J. Thuss. LHA

Left, inset—*This group of men struck a pose at the tomb before the 1883 installation of the iron railing.* LHA

Above, top—*On October 22, 1907, Mrs. Mary C. Dorris, Regent, stood beside President Theodore Roosevelt at the tomb. Afterwards, three thousand people crowded the speaker's stand to hear his remarks.* H. O. Fuller. LHA

Above—*President and Mrs. Lyndon B. Johnson laid a wreath at the tomb of Andrew Jackson on his 200th birthday, March 15, 1967.* Vic Cooley. LHA

23

THE HERMITAGE LANDSCAPE

Above—*Pleasant coolness on a summer's day at the tomb in 1997.* LHA

Right—*The mighty hickories fallen. 4/18/98.* MM

Far right, top—*Magnolia branches knocked down family gravestones. Unscathed was Dr. John Lawrence's tombstone, designed in the form of a broken tree. 5/5/98.* JTH

Far right, bottom—*The tomb can barely be seen through the debris of toppled trees covering the garden. 4/18/98.* MM

Left—*The gate and 115-year-old railing were broken apart by the impact of the falling magnolia. Directly behind the tomb was the former location of the hickory trees. 5/5/98.* JTH

Left, bottom—*Alfred Jackson's tombstone barely missed being smashed by the collapse of the hickory trees. 4/17/98.* KD

Below—*The tomb, undamaged in the tornado, continues to be a place of pilgrimage. 9/26/98.* JTH

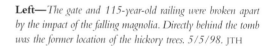

It was amazing that the tomb was not hit because those five hickories fell like tooth-picks, side by side. The magnolia fell on the other side. It was like there was an invisible safety net around the tomb. Some of the family tombstones were knocked down by ends of branches but they were not smashed.

Karen Danielson,
gardener,
great-great-great-great-great-granddaughter of
President Jackson

When I finally got to the mansion, the very first person that I saw was Mark Provost (Buildings & Grounds head, 1998). Mark was standing by the garden gate and he was practically in tears. The first thing that he said to me, "Everything has changed." And basically he was right. The garden, around the tomb was awful. . . . I really think someone was looking out for the general's tomb.

Tony Guzzi,
curatorial assistant

PART THREE

In Andrew Jackson's day, the property surrounding the Hermitage was a busy place, full of the daily activities of running a household and the farm. Still in existence today are the well, kitchen, smokehouse, and one dwelling called Alfred's Cabin. Long gone are other buildings such as the icehouse, slave dwellings as well as wash and weaving houses, henhouses, and the fences which separated these buildings from the fields beyond.

The Backyard

Mrs. Mary C. Dorris, LHA Board member, in 1896 described the backyard as "utterly devoid of trees." The planting of trees was an objective during the early days of the LHA management. Trees were needed to reduce summer heat inside the mansion and to cool the porches and walkways. Shade was essential for the visiting public.

In 1901, the board accepted a bid for $75 to plant two hundred trees, hydrangeas, and a bed of roses. In 1911, Miss Louise Lindsley, Regent, reported the successful planting of over one hundred trees in the front and back lawns. Trees often were described as "diseased." In 1913, the "Original Tree Doctor and Surgeon" was paid $800 to treat the trees around the house and on the lawns.

Alfred Jackson was living on the Hermitage grounds when the LHA took over management in 1889. According to Mrs. Mary C. Dorris, in her book, *Preservation of the Hermitage,* published in 1915, Alfred was born a slave on the Hermitage farm:

Uncle Alfred had never lived anywhere but at the Hermitage. His life was bounded by its horizon. He was born there, lived there, died there, and was buried there by the Association. He had witnessed the changes through nearly a century of time, for he was ninety-eight years old when he died.

After her marriage to Andrew Jackson Jr. in 1831, Sarah York Jackson brought Gracey, a slave, with her to The Hermitage. Alfred and Gracey were wed and continued to live on the place even after the conclusion of the Civil War. Gracey died before the formation of the Ladies' Hermitage Association. Alfred served as guide to visitors and occupied the cabin in the backyard until his death in 1901. The LHA held his funeral in the front hall of the mansion and he was buried just north of the tomb of President and Mrs. Jackson.

In the early 1900s, the LHA had begun to use the backyard for their membership outings and for special occasions. Secretary of War Jacob McGavock Dickinson, a Nashville native, was given a barbecue on June 21, 1910. The president's granddaughter, Rachel Jackson Lawrence, age seventy-seven, attended. From Nashville, the guests were conveyed the twelve miles to The Hermitage in automobiles and horse-drawn tallyhos.

On November 11, 1914, Mrs. B. F. Wilson, Regent, and Mrs. Guilford Dudley, president of the local suffrage league, were on hand to welcome delegates to the National Equal Suffrage League Convention. The local newspaper described the event:

A barbecue and a sumptuous luncheon was served under the forest trees on the rear lawn. The decorations of the table artistically developed the rustic idea. Autumn leaves, rich-hued fruits and berries ornamented the board, together with banners bearing the inscription "Votes for Women."

To better understand the backyard, archaeological investigation has been conducted. Dr. Larry McKee, staff archaeologist, reported in 1988:

Excavation around the exterior of the garden's northwest corner unexpectedly uncovered a stone chimney base and small brick-lined root cellar, remains of a slave dwelling located less than 150 feet from the back door of the mansion.

From 1988 to 1998, extensive archaeological investigation revealed additional structures in the backyard, including a three-unit slave dwelling, an icehouse, a kiln for making bricks, sets of fences which bounded the backyard, and antebellum period artifacts associated with the slave dwellings. According to Larry McKee, as many as thirty or forty enslaved persons lived in the backyard area.

The Church

On land donated by Andrew Jackson, a church was built with funds raised "by subscription" from him and his neighbors. Bricks were made in the kiln on the Hermitage farm. Rachel Jackson, a charter member, attended this church, called "Ephesus," from 1824 until her death in 1828. After retiring from the presidency, Jackson and his daughter-in-law, Sarah York Jackson, joined the church on July 15, 1838. The next year, the Nashville Presbytery changed the name of the church to "Hermitage" in honor of Andrew Jackson.

General Jackson is very feeble, much bent, his hair long and white. I observed he holds in his hands a very old Hymn-book, which I found on inquiry was one which belonged to his wife. . . . His spectacles, cane, a broad brimmed white hat with its band of crepe put one in mind of the many caricatures of the General.

School Master,
July 25, 1844

Many old-timers remembered the president coming early to light the fire during the winter, tying his horse to a tree near the front door of the church. A stump of this tree stood until the tornado of 1998.

The church was a part of the Jackson family in many ways. Two months after his father's death, Andrew Jackson Jr. joined the church. The next year, he was made an elder, a position he held until his death in 1865. Sarah and Andrew Jackson Jr.'s daughter, Rachel Jackson Lawrence, joined in 1867. She was a faithful Sunday school teacher and member for the rest of her life, for fifty-six years.

After the Civil War, E. D. Finney boarded at the Hermitage, where Sarah Jackson and her sister Marion Adams were living. He was "preaching and teaching."

> I have a large congregation to preach to every Sabbath—very attentive & very anxious for preaching—having had none during the war. . . . The people promise me about $1500 a year, out of that I pay my board, which is $1 per day.
>
> E. D. Finney,
> October 18, 1866

Amy Rich of Cincinnati, Ohio, moved to the neighborhood to teach school after the Civil War. She fell in love with Andrew Jackson III. After their marriage, they became the last tenants-at-will living at The Hermitage. The Hermitage was opened to the public on July 17, 1889. Jackson III and his family departed four years later. Andrew Jackson III died in Knoxville in 1906. Memorial services were held for him in the old Hermitage Church followed by burial in the family plot near President Jackson's tomb.

On February 20, 1965, the church was gutted by fire. After this disaster, the congregation, responding to a longtime wish of the Ladies' Hermitage Association, transferred the title to the property to the LHA, in exchange for nearby land and funds towards construction of a new Hermitage Presbyterian Church. Four years later, a special service marked the restoration of the old Hermitage Church. Mrs. Douglas Henry, LHA Board member, served as the restoration project chairman. Today, the church is interpreted as part of the historic Hermitage properties and often is used for special services and for weddings.

In 1892, on Hermitage land, the State of Tennessee officially opened the new Confederate Soldiers' Home built to provide for indigent veterans. A cemetery was developed near the Hermitage Church and 487 CSA veterans were buried there before the closing of the soldier's home in 1933. Ralph Ledbetter, an African-American slave who accompanied his owner to war, is also buried there. Descendants of these veterans continue to visit the cemetery. In 1935, the State of Tennessee conveyed additional acres of the original Hermitage property, including the cemetery, to the care of the LHA.

In 1948, the Hermitage Presbyterian Church agreed to set aside land near the church as a cemetery for the Donelson family. Under the supervision of Mrs. Gilbert S. Merritt, LHA Board member, the relocation of tombstones and reinterments were carried out for Emily Donelson, who had lived at Tulip Grove; her parents, Mary and John Donelson; Severn and Elizabeth Donelson, parents of Andrew Jackson Jr.; and other members of the Donelson family. Today the Donelson Family Cemetery is maintained as part of the historic Hermitage properties.

Tulip Grove

Andrew Jackson helped to finance the construction of a new Greek Revival house for Emily and Andrew Jackson Donelson located across the pike from his own home. Rachel Jackson was aunt to both Emily and A. J. Donelson. Joseph Reiff and William C. Hume, engaged in rebuilding the Hermitage after the 1834 fire, also built the Donelson residence. Before the house was finished, the Donelsons were corresponding about plans for their lawn and garden.

> My idea is that the garden should be in rear of the House and that the handsome plat in front of the House should be enclosed by two lines of fence connecting with the paling of the yard affording space enough for a circular turn for carriages.
>
> Andrew Jackson Donelson,
> to his wife, May 10, 1835

During Jackson's presidency, Emily Donelson served as hostess of the President's House for almost seven years. In the summer of 1836, the Donelsons were happy to leave Washington and move into their newly completed house.

A few months later, Emily was unable to return to Washington because of ill health. She was suffering from tuberculosis. Her husband, as the president's private secretary, had to go back to Washington. When Donelson returned home on December 22, he learned Emily had died three days before. In 1841, Donelson married his second cousin, Elizabeth Anderson Martin Randolph, a young widow. She was fond of his four children and they were to have eight children of their own.

In 1842, at the suggestion of visiting President Martin Van Buren, the name of the house was changed from Poplar Grove to Tulip Grove. The splendid tulip poplars grew ever more handsome as the years went along until the tornado of 1998.

A. J. Donelson returned to government service, serving as minister to Prussia during the administration of James K. Polk. Following an unsuccessful bid for the vice-presidency on the American Party ticket in the election of 1856, Donelson returned to Tulip Grove. By this time, The Hermitage had been sold to the state. Two years later, in 1858, Donelson sold Tulip Grove and moved with his family to Memphis, Tennessee. He practiced law until his death in 1871, at age seventy-two.

In the years following the sale, Tulip Grove saw a number of caring owners, including the Cockrills, Treanors, and Buntins. Since 1965, Tulip Grove has been open for visitors as a part of the historic Hermitage properties.

Above—*Aerial view directly over the one-acre garden and the mansion. By the date of this photograph, the garden had been cleaned of all debris. 4/24/98.* JTH

Right—*Tumbled trees near Alfred's Cabin in the backyard. 4/24/98.* JTH

Opposite—*Tree branches crashed down on the cellar door where visitors and staff had taken refuge during the tornado. 4/17/98.* TG

30

And it was over. Then we could not get out. It took three men pushing from the inside and they literally just broke the door off its hinges for us to get out. I was the last person out. Marsha Mullin was already there. She said, "The mansion is okay."

Angie Nichols,
executive assistant

They had to push the cellar doors open. A whole tree was on the cellar doors. Finally we let all the visitors out. They were climbing over trees. Shock. Absolute shock. We were looking around and not knowing what we were looking at. At the back of the house, trees were everywhere.

John Lamb,
lead interpreter

Opposite, far left—*This twisted cedar is evidence of the awesome power of the tornado. 4/24/98.* JTH

Opposite, top—*A garden view from the front balcony of the mansion. The tomb stands alone. In the distance one can see the path of the tornado. 5/5/98.* JTH

Opposite, bottom—*Junior docents participated in the Harvest Fair at The Hermitage. The return of normalcy. 9/26/98.* JTH

Left, top—*Archaeologist Dr. Larry McKee and volunteer Susan Hollyday examined one of over 1,200 tree craters for any artifacts in the soil or around roots. 5/5/98.* JTH

Left, bottom—*Everyone on The Hermitage staff pitched in and helped remove the seemingly endless number of tree limbs. 5/5/98.* JTH

When I first saw the church, I was devastated. It looked like someone had taken a bulldozer and piled every one of our trees in a pile. I thought will we ever have weddings there again? Five months later, on October 24, was the first wedding held in the church since the tornado.

Yvonne Wheeler,
visitors services manager

I was amazed how many trees could fall and how few of them strike a building. The face of the church got hit hard but it was really superficial damage—nothing that could not be repaired. We did not lose anything. Some chimneys were broken but could be rebricked. I am amazed that many trees could fall and not hurt anybody. We did not have an injury.

Richard Bartley,
maintenance department

Above—*"The Church Where Jackson Worships" is the title of this lithograph. Andrew Jackson joined this Presbyterian Church in 1838.* Prudhomme. Hillyer. TSLA

Right—*The Hermitage Presbyterian Church was gutted by fire in 1965. Mrs. Douglas Henry, the LHA Church Restoration Chairman, was present for the reopening service on May 21, 1969.* LHA

Far left—*The force of the wind ripped off the top of this huge tree. 4/24/98.* JTH

Above—*Above the front doors of the church, a falling tree crushed part of the roof and chimney. Trees were strewn all around the churchyard. 4/24/98.* JTH

Left—*Some of the Donelson family gravestones were damaged in the cemetery beside the church. 4/24/98.* JTH

Above—*The Greek Revival facade of Tulip Grove is totally obscured by uprooted trees on the lawn. 4/24/98.* JTH

Opposite, far left—*Tulip Grove was spared direct injury when this tree fell sideways. 4/24/98.* JTH

Opposite, top—*Tulip Grove, home of Andrew Jackson Donelson, was built in 1836. The house was opened to the public in 1965, as a part of the historic Hermitage properties, 1985.* LHA

Opposite, bottom—*Aerial view over the lawn of destroyed tulip poplar trees at Tulip Grove. 4/24/98.* JTH

Following page—*Nineteenth-century engraving depicts President Jackson in the carriage drive.* Prudhomme. Hillyer. TSLA

At first I started walking up Rachel's Lane to Tulip Grove, but I realized that was useless so I went out to the fields. I forgot there was a wet spring and I got soaked about up to my waist before I realized what was happening.

Raymond Johnson,
co-chief of security

On Tuesday afternoon before the tornado, my aunt Willie D. Buntin and I had driven up around Tulip Grove so I had a picture of the way everything was in my mind, and remember thinking "this is beautiful." But driving there out Lebanon Road on Friday after the tornado, it was just the opposite. It was amazing. It looked like there had been a battle there. It was unbelievable.

Mary N. Wade,
Regent 1997–1998

I looked down Rachel's Lane and saw how devastated it was. It seemed to me, at the time, that there was not a tree standing all the way to Tulip Grove. It was a jumble. We had to remove fence sections to get people out of Tulip Grove, and it took two days to clear a fire lane to Tulip Grove.

Jim Vaughan,
executive director

Everything at the Hermitage bears the impress of the General's character—
all is on a large scale and of a useful and magnanimous caste.

Visit of Francis P. Blair,

May 14, 1842

Niles National Register

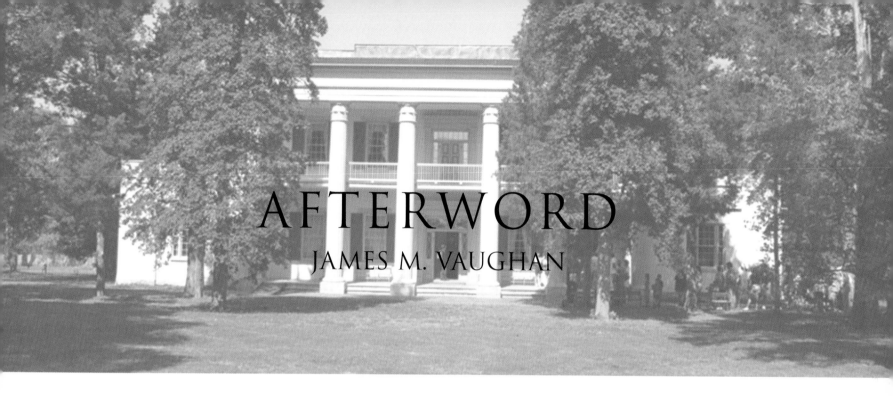

AFTERWORD

JAMES M. VAUGHAN

The beautiful landscape at The Hermitage has always been an important part of the visitor experience. But some of the Hermitage landscape dates from the nineteenth century and some from the twentieth. In February 1998, two months prior to the tornado, the Hermitage Board of Directors adopted a plan to undertake a multiyear project to research, preserve, and restore the Hermitage landscape to a more appropriate nineteenth-century appearance. We had just completed a ten-year effort to restore the Hermitage mansion interiors to their appearance in Jackson's day and felt we should now address the grounds with an equal commitment to history. We knew that many additional years of historical and archaeological research would be required to develop a comprehensive and historically based landscape plan. We also recognized that many of our present landscape elements which dated from the early twentieth century were reaching the end of their natural life cycle. It seemed an ideal time to begin such a major research project.

The tornado of April 16 has not altered our plans. It has only increased the need for careful historical analysis. Thus, throughout the crisis and cleanup, we remained focused on the need to protect and record all the historical information that will be needed to restore the Hermitage landscape.

In the days, weeks, and months following the tornado, the Hermitage staff also learned many lessons that could be of value to others who are hit by a tornado, hurricane, ice storm, or other weather emergency.

First, prior disaster planning was a key element in minimizing our loss at the time of the tornado and in speeding our recovery afterwards. Our written disaster plan, developed several years ago, included a chain of command, emergency job descriptions with clear responsibilities, a communications tree, and specified locations for emergency supplies. Our emergency training included practice evacuation drills with visitors on the premises, which may have been responsible for the fact that no one was killed or injured during the tornado at The Hermitage. This preplanning proved critical because it allowed us to respond quickly according to preestablished responsibilities. In the few chaotic hours after the tornado, we tended to all the emergency needs of staff, visitors, and property without a single meeting of the staff to determine what needed to be done.

Our emergency planning was based on the premise that we could not depend on any outside help from public emergency services such as fire, police, or even local utility companies, during the first few hours of an emergency. On April 16, tornado and storm damage were widespread throughout Middle Tennessee. Although Hermitage security quickly established radio communication with Metro Police, there was little outside assistance during the first twenty-four hours and to a large degree the first three or four days.

Equally important to our recovery, and particularly so during the first few days, was the decision to assign highest priority to the preservation of historic and archaeological resources over cost and speed. We quickly contacted other historic sites that had experienced natural disasters for advice and they stressed the importance of proceeding carefully and of monitoring the work of all outside contractors to assure that cleanup work did not endanger historic and archaeological resources. Implementing their recommendations, we prohibited the use of any tracked vehicles such as bulldozers because of the severe damage they would do to our archaeological resources, and delayed the removal of stumps until archaeological examinations were complete. The staff completed much of the cleanup around the mansion and garden by hand, and we concentrated our large equipment on roads where they could operate on hard surfaces. Although this did not always allow us to be working in the areas we most wanted to clean up, it did prevent additional damage.

The preservation of the remaining trees and landscape materials was also a high priority. Morris Arboretum of the University of Pennsylvania generously loaned us three arborists for a week to assess damage to standing trees and to help us conserve those that could be saved. Our neighbors from Cheekwood sent a large crew for a day to help us and to remove debris from the Hermitage garden.

Our preservation priorities also led us to attempt to salvage as much valuable and historic lumber from the downed trees as possible. Within the first few days, a team from the State of Tennessee Department of Forestry had marked downed trees that might have potential value as lumber. We quickly registered our lumber with the Smart Wood program, an international organization which certifies that lumber has not been clear-cut or harvested in an environmentally unfriendly manner.

The third element that guided us throughout the emergency and the recovery operation was the rapid development and implementation of a financial/business plan to steer us through the entire recovery period. It would be hard to overstate the potentially negative financial impact of a major disaster on an organization like The Hermitage which draws more than 90 percent of its annual operating revenues from visitor admissions and sales. Our financial recovery plan was completed within the first few weeks following the tornado, although it was constantly reviewed and amended throughout the recovery period. As was the case with the emergency planning, several of the most important elements were actually in place before the tornado struck.

As part of our overall financial planning, we have regularly reviewed our insurance coverage. We had added insurance coverage for loss of business revenue several years ago. Thus, even though we were closed for a month, we kept full staff on the payroll. This allowed us to reopen more quickly because staff were paid to assist in the recovery effort.

Many components of the plan were developed immediately after the tornado. Foremost among these was the development of a public relations, marketing, and development plan. At the outset, we agreed that we did not want to compete for attention or funds with the many families who had suffered tornado damage in east Nashville and elsewhere. Therefore, we decided not to launch a public appeal for funds, but rather to rely primarily on a mailed special addition of our newsletter to inform the members about the extent of damage and to provide them with an opportunity to make a contribution. We eventually received in excess of $80,000 for the tornado recovery from this simple mailing. From the beginning, all of our efforts stressed the eventual reopening and that the historic structures themselves had sustained only minimal damage. We completed a national press release and within a few days news of the damage at The Hermitage had been spread from coast to coast. We knew it would be more difficult to receive national attention for our reopening, and thus, we began to plan reopening ceremonies and a series of media events long before a reopening date had even been established.

We began discussions with representatives of the Federal Emergency Management Agency (FEMA) and the Tennessee Emergency Management Agency (TEMA) almost immediately after the tornado, and by June had determined the potential maximum amounts of federal assistance that would be available to us, and then negotiated contracts with our principal outside contractor.

The final part of our financial and business plan was to explore a variety of possible opportunities to generate recovery funds from the sale of lumber or the production of specialized merchandise from the downed trees. We worked to assure that most of the wood was harvested or recycled. We gave tulip poplar and hickory to the Gibson Guitar Company which produced a limited edition of Hermitage guitars for collectors. They donated ten of these guitars to The Hermitage and the proceeds from their sale will be used to offset some of the Hermitage recovery expenses. Similar arrangements with individual craftsmen have produced a number of commemorative rocking chairs, cradles, bowls, and many smaller items which are generating revenue and allowing some of this historic wood to be appropriately preserved.

The tornado of April 16 lasted less than a minute, but the recovery was the central element in Hermitage operations for an entire year. No doubt landscape restoration will take many years but, in most other areas, Hermitage operations returned to normal before the first anniversary date of the tornado. Despite being closed for more than a month, and despite the two million-dollar costs of cleanup and restoration, The Hermitage completed both the year of the tornado and the year of recovery in the black. Our continuous commitment to preserving and recording archaeological, historical, and landscape information throughout the cleanup and recovery process allows us to move forward with our plans to research and restore the grounds to their nineteenth-century appearance during the age of Andrew Jackson.

APPENDIX I

NATIONAL PARK SERVICE SATELLITE MAPPING

Although many of the trees destroyed in the storm dated from the twentieth century, a number also dated from Jackson's time. Thus, it was important to record information about each lost tree. The National Park Service sent a team of three specialists who worked alongside staff and volunteers to record the precise location, the species, and the circumference of every downed and damaged tree, as well as those left standing. Using computers and satellite receivers, each tree on the property was located using global positioning system technology. This data has produced detailed maps of the Hermitage landscape before and after the tornado.

INITIAL SURVEY AREA	RESULTS
Individual trees mapped:	2,038
Down or severely damaged:	944
Red cedars:	296 lost
Tulip poplars:	174 lost
Sugar maples:	121 lost
Last of old hickory trees:	lost

Average circumference of standing trees
Before the tornado:	6.05 feet
After the tornado:	2.86 feet

Opposite and below—*Global positioning system maps of The Hermitage trees before (opposite) and after (below) the tornado of April 16, 1998.* NPS

Right—*A member of the National Park Service conducts satellite mapping at The Hermitage.* CA

APPENDIX II

REFERENCES

COLLECTIONS

The Papers of Andrew Jackson, University of
Tennessee, Knoxville

*The Papers of Andrew Jackson, Guide and Index to the
Microfilm Edition,* 1979, Harold D. Moser, ed.

Ladies' Hermitage Association, Hermitage,
Tennessee
- Minutes and annual reports
- Papers

Preservation of the Hermitage, 1889–1915, Mary C.
Dorris, self-published.

Diary of Mary Elizabeth Lewis Dufield, May 14,
1851. Courtesy of Mrs. Mary Bradford.

LIBRARY OF CONGRESS

A. J. Donelson Papers

Andrew Jackson Papers

METROPOLITAN ARCHIVES

TENNESSEE STATE LIBRARY AND ARCHIVES

NEWSPAPERS

New York Times
Cincinnati Commercial Tribune
Nashville Union
Nashville Republican
Boston Post
Nashville Union and American
Niles National Register

BOOKS

Georgian at Princeton
Children of Pride
Senate Journal, February 22, 1883

PHOTO CREDITS

AC — Anna Christ, 12

CA — Clare Adams, 43

FC — Fletch Coke, 5, 20, 21

JTH — John T. Hooper, 4, 5, 6, 9, 10,11, 12, 13,
20, 21, 24, 25, 30, 32, 33, 35, 36, 37

KD — Karen Danielson, 5, 25

LHA — Ladies' Hermitage Association, xii, 5, 6,
8, 10, 12, 18, 23, 24, 34, 36, 43

MM — Marsha Mullin, 24

NPS — National Park Service, 42, 43

NR — Nashville Room Public Library, 7

TG — Tony Guzzi, 31

TSLA — Tennessee State Library and Archives, 8,
9, 19, 34, 38

APPENDIX III

VISITING THE HERMITAGE

Location:	Rachel's Lane, Hermitage, Tennessee (near Nashville)
Directions:	Exit 221, I-40
Hours:	Open daily from 9 A.M. to 5 P.M.
Closed:	Thanksgiving and Christmas days and the third week of January
Group rates:	Available for groups of twenty or more with advance reservations
Tour includes:	Film, museum, Hermitage mansion, garden, self-guided archaeology tour, Jackson's tomb, original log cabins, Old Hermitage Church, Tulip Grove mansion, and the Confederate cemetery. Audio tour of mansion, interpreters in mansion provide additional information.
Information:	(615) 889-2941 or www.thehermitage.com

LADIES' HERMITAGE ASSOCIAITON

The Ladies' Hermitage Association (LHA) is a private not-for-profit organization chartered by the State of Tennessee in 1889. The mission of the LHA is to preserve and interpret to the public the buildings, grounds, and artifacts related to the life and times of President Andrew Jackson in order that the legacy of his life and times might serve as a resource, guide, and inspiration for future generation in order that they might better understand the principles of democracy and the history and development of the United States. The LHA is a membership organization open to all.

TENNESSEE PRESIDENTS TRUST

The Tennessee Presidents Trust supports publishing the papers of the three Tennessee presidents and fostering a greater appreciation of their legacy to American democracy. The trust includes the papers of Andrew Jackson, established by the LHA in 1970; the correspondence of James K. Polk; and the papers of Andrew Johnson. To date, five volumes of Jackson's papers have been published. For more information about these scholarly publications and related research interests, contact the Trust Director, Hoskins Library 216, University of Tennessee, Knoxville, TN 37996-4000.

ANDREW JACKSON & HIS FAMILY AT
THE HERMITAGE

1760   1765   1770   1775   1780   1785   1790   1795   1800   1805   1810   1815   1820   1825

1767

◆1767, March 15
Andrew Jackson, third son of Andrew and Elizabeth (Hutchinson) Jackson, is born in Waxhaws, South Carolina.

◆1784–1786
Jackson studies law under Spruce McCay in Salisbury, North Carolina.

◆1788, October
Andrew Jackson, a young attorney, settles in Nashville.

◆1796, March 10
Jackson purchases Hunter's Hill farm in Davidson County, Tennessee. Jackson will sell the farm in July 1804.

◆1796, October 22
Jackson is elected to represent Tennessee in the U.S. Congress as a member of the House of Representatives. In less than a year, Tennessee will again elect Jackson, this time as a U.S. Senator on September 26, 1797.

◆1804, August 23
Jackson purchases the Hermitage property and moves into a two-story log building.

◆1806, May 30
Jackson duels with Charles Dickinson at Red River, Logan County Kentucky. Dickinson is killed and Jackson is severely wounded.

◆1794, January 18
In Nashville, Rachel and Andrew Jackson marry for the second time.

◆1791, August
Rachel Donelson and Andrew Jackson marry, for the first time, in Natchez, which was Spanish Territory.

◆1785, March
Rachel Donelson marries Lewis Robards in Kentucky.

◆1780, April 24
Col. John Donelson leads a flotilla of boats with pioneer settlers, including his twelve-year-old daughter Rachel, to found what would eventually become Nashville.

◆1767
Rachel Donelson, the youngest daughter and eighth of eleven children of John and Rachel (Stockley) Donelson, is born in Pittsylvania County, Virginia.

◆1790, December 20
Lewis Robards is granted permission to sue for divorce in Kentucky District (not yet a state) by Virginia Legislature. He does not file suit until 1792. The divorce is finally granted September 27, 1793.

1828, November
Andrew Jackson is elected U[S] president.

◆1819, summer
Construction of a ne[w] brick house begins on T[he] Hermitage property. T[he] Jacksons will return [to] their newly complet[ed] house November 4, 182[1] after he serves as ter[ri]torial governor of Flori[da].

◆1814, May 28
Jackson is commissioned major general of the United States Army by President James Madison.

◆1815, January 8
General Jackson wins Battle of Orleans over British. Dubbed "[Hero] of Battle of New Orleans."

◆1808, December 4
Rachel's sister-in-law, Elizabeth Donelson, has twins. The Jacksons "adopt" one of the twins and name him Andrew Jackson Jr.

1824 ◆
Ephesus Church is dedicated.

1767-1893

1830 · 1835 · 1840 · 1845 · 1850 · 1855 · 1860 · 1865 · 1870 · 1875 · 1880 · 1885 · 1890 · 1895

◆**1845, June 8**
Andrew Jackson, age 78, dies at The Hermitage.

◆**1856, February 11**
The State of Tennessee purchases five hundred acres of the Hermitage farm, including the mansion and tomb, for $48,000 from Andrew Jackson Jr.

◆**1889**
On February 19, the Ladies' Hermitage Association is chartered. The State of Tennessee turns over twenty-five acres, including the mansion and tomb, to the LHA on April 5. On July 17 the LHA opens The Hermitage to the public.

◆**1828, December 22**
Rachel Jackson dies at The Hermitage. Two days later, her funeral oration is given by the Reverend William Hume and she becomes the first person to be buried in the garden at The Hermitage.

◆**1845, June 10**
Jackson's funeral is held at The Hermitage. He is buried in the garden, beside his wife Rachel. His funeral oration is preached by the Reverend John Todd Edgar.

◆**1859**
Governor Isham Harris invites Sarah and Andrew Jackson Jr. to live at The Hermitage as tenants-at-will.

◆**1833**
The tomb, designed by Nashville architect David Morison, is completed in the garden.

◆**1861**
Andrew Jackson III and his brother Samuel enlist in the Confederate Army. Samuel will die from wounds he suffers at the Battle of Chickamauga. Col. Andrew Jackson III is captured and imprisoned during the war. Upon his release, he will return and live at The Hermitage.

◆**1829**
On January 19, Andrew Jackson departs for his inauguration in Washington City. On March 4, he takes the oath of office and becomes the seventh president of the United States, the first president from the "West."

◆**1865, April 17**
Andrew Jackson Jr. dies from lockjaw after a hunting accident at The Hermitage.

◆**1833, March 4**
Jackson is inaugurated for his second term as president.

◆**1877, October 15**
Andrew Jackson III marries Amy Rich. They will have two sons, Andrew Jackson IV and Albert Marble Preston Jackson, both born at The Hermitage.

◆**1834, October 13**
The Hermitage mansion is partially destroyed by fire.

◆**1837, March 25**
Jackson returns home to his newly rebuilt and refurbished mansion.

1887, August 23 ◆
Sarah York Jackson dies at The Hermitage.

◆**1831, November 24**
Andrew Jackson Jr. and Sarah York marry at the First Presbyterian Church in Philadelphia, Pennsylvania.

◆**1832–1837**
Rachel, Andrew III, and Samuel Jackson are born to Sarah and Andrew Jackson Jr. at The Hermitage.

1893 ◆
Andrew Jackson III, wife Amy, and sons Andrew Jackson IV and Albert Marble Preston Jackson, depart from The Hermitage.

1893

THE CIVIL WAR 1861–1865

ABOUT THE AUTHOR

Fletch Coke became involved in historic preservation in the mid-1970s. Since that time, she has served as a member of the Metro Historical Commission; president of Historic Nashville, Inc.; president of the Union Station Trust Fund; and board member and Regent of the Ladies' Hermitage Association. Currently, she serves as the archivist for the Episcopal Diocese of Tennessee and president of the Board of Governors of the Tennessee Presidents Trust. Fletch is also currently involved in research and writing about Judge John Overton of Travellers Rest, Christ Church Cathedral in Nashville, and Union Station.

Fletch Coke is a graduate of Holton-Arms School, Washington, D.C. She received a bachelor of arts degree in history and a master of science degree in speech pathology and audiology from Vanderbilt University. She is married to William G. Coke Jr., and is the mother of two grown daughters.

SPECIAL THANKS

The author wishes to offer special thanks to Honey Rodgers and Jim Vaughan for their initial response to the idea of a tornado book; Marsha Mullin and Tony Guzzi, curatorial staff at The Hermitage; the keen eye of photographer John T. Hooper; Providence House Publishers, especially Andrew Miller, Mary Bray Wheeler, Debbie Sims, and Stephen James for their help in the development and production of this book.